THE WAY OF THE SOUL®

HOW TO CREATE INSTANT MAGIC IN A BUSY LIFE

We all tend to live such busy lives - no time for ourselves or one another. Bring back the MAGIC in your life.

Author Ross Bonacci ©

Artist Poona ©

Registered® The Way Of The Soul 2011 All Rights Reserved

www.thewayofthesoul.com

Copyright © 2011 Ross Bonacci

All rights reserved. No part of this book may be used or reproduced by any means, graphic, electronic, or mechanical, including photocopying, recording, taping or by any information storage retrieval system without the written permission of the publisher except in the case of brief quotations embodied in critical articles and reviews.

ISBN: 978-1-4525-3823-5

Library of Congress Control Number: 2011915024

Balboa Press books may be ordered through booksellers or by contacting:

*Balboa Press
A Division of Hay House
1663 Liberty Drive
Bloomington, IN 47403
www.balboapress.com
1-(877) 407-4847*

Because of the dynamic nature of the Internet, any web addresses or links contained in this book may have changed since publication and may no longer be valid. The views expressed in this work are solely those of the author and do not necessarily reflect the views of the publisher, and the publisher hereby disclaims any responsibility for them.

Any people depicted in stock imagery provided by Thinkstock are models, and such images are being used for illustrative purposes only. Certain stock imagery © Thinkstock.

The views expressed in this work are solely those of the author and do not necessarily reflect the views of the publisher, and the publisher hereby disclaims any responsibility for them.

Printed in the United States of America

Balboa Press rev. date: 9/14/2011

ROSS BONACCI / FOUNDER

THE WAY OF THE SOUL – about the author

Ross Bonacci has studied and explored numerous healing modalities and is a Master of Reiki, Zenith Omega, and Avatar. He has been on the path of self-discovery since his late teens and his great appreciation for life has inspired an enquiry into the human potential. He confesses his soul guided him on his travels.

His journey has taken him many sacred places both within himself and also geographical locations around the world. He embraces a multi-denominational view point on the Cosmos and all that is.

The Way of the Soul is the distillation of his many trainings and his experiential understanding of them. Ross humbly, yet proudly, now presents to you his offering of thanks to all those who have been part of his evolution. How To Create Instant Magic in a Busy Life is his gift to you to honor and accelerate your journey home to yourself.

Ross lives in Sydney, Australia.
He is available for private consultations and trainings.

Thank you

From the bottom of my heart I thank you for purchasing How To Create Instant Magic in a Busy Life. It is my absolute privilege and pleasure to present this book to you. It will help you expand your mind and give you a deeper understanding of the human journey.

Acknowledgment

A very special thank you goes to Poona for her loving guidance and creative inspiration. Poona is a truly gifted artist who was guided to me by God. Her art work is truly amazing.

Thank you to Ali Inayat and Vanessa Simmonds for their insightful inspiration.

The acknowledgement is not complete without mention of Raihnon. He has been instrumental in my learning and helped profoundly with piecing everything together.

Ross Bonacci - Founder of The Way of the Soul

THE INSPIRATION

What has happened to humanity?

Fear is running riot. There are so many people out there asking for help. We live in neighborhoods where no one knows each other. The elderly are too afraid to leave their own homes. Some people have lost all hope. Many people live their lives filled with anger and resentment. These days, depression is accepted as a familiar word. Compulsive addictions and emotional disorders are more common.

Gee... this sounds so bad. What has happened to humanity?
Is this as bad as it will get, or is the worst yet to come?

Well, who knows? You are a product of your past – it is <u>your</u> past actions that have made you into who you are today. As you begin to study How To Create Instant Magic in a Busy Life, you already begin to disentangle yourself from the negative programming that has affected you in your life. In most cases, this was just something someone said to you, which you then took onboard as your truth.

Take a moment to check - are you living someone else's truth, or is it yours? What unhelpful programs have you permitted to be installed within yourself? Allow yourself to install new joyful, uplifting programming. See yourself as a computer that is getting a major software upgrade. How To Create Instant Magic in a Busy Life will assist you in upgrading the files in your mind.

An educated, logical and positive mind is a powerful one!

WHO IS LUCY?

As you gaze upon these images you will meet Lucy and her friends who help you understand the teachings through their journey in the images.

But who is Lucy?

Lucy is an Angel; who lives in the angelic realms.

Lucy will be the light that helps you see and understand the truth behind the teachings

WHAT IS THIS BOOK ABOUT?

How To Create Instant Magic in a Busy Life is an educational tool to help you understand human behavior.

As you read these insightful messages and gaze upon these amazing images, you begin to explore and understand new concepts and new view-points on the human condition.

You must reflect the understanding you gain from this book into your own life.

Each time you read a message and gaze upon an image, it gives you new tools to understand yourself. The messages will help you see beyond your own deceptions and self-imposed limitations; and they allow your mind to expand to a new level of being.

**Each message carries a compelling heartfelt 'Intention' for you to feel at the core of your being.
This 'Intention' is amplified with a new command statement labeled
*'The Message and You'***

Absorb the messages and life as you know it will change; just as the caterpillar transforms into the beautiful butterfly. You will also begin to remember; embracing, reconnecting and reigniting the brilliance of your true essence.

YOU HAVE THE POWER TO CREATE MAGIC IN YOUR LIFE

ADVENTURE

You are going on an adventure. You are off to see the world!

All pain, suffering and worrying, ends for you right <u>now</u>.

Today is the beginning of a new day.
Each day is a new adventure!

What will this day bring to you? Who knows - this is a day you haven't lived before.
It's an adventure, a new beginning!

Start your day like you have started your life anew. Be like a carefree, passionate wanderer as you set off into the dawn, ready for what life will throw at you!

Open your eyes. Allow yourself to see the love and beauty in all things. Your life is a wonderful expression of divinity. You are part of all there is. As you lovingly gaze with new eyes from deep within you, you see the beauty in all things. Your daily life becomes a wondrous adventure!

**Intention:
I gracefully embrace the wonders of each new day.
My life is a wonderful adventure!**

The Message and You:
You are a pioneer.

ADVENTURE

You are a pioneer

ANGELS

We give you guidance from beyond.

We are the unseen helpers of God.

The beloved Angels are with you always, whether or not you are aware of it. Believe it; the Angels watch you from afar.

They send you loving guidance and are highly skilled in keeping you safe.

Call upon an Angel when you feel the need. More often than not, we will not ask for help or accept help when it is given. We are too proud, too stubborn; or we falsely think we have to do it alone and separate ourselves from others.

Ask and you shall receive.
Learn to accept that it is okay to ask for help whether it is from an Angel, friend or family. It takes great courage to know when you need help and then to ask for it. Sometimes, when you ask an Angel for help, a new person enters your life and gives you all the help and support you require.

Take a moment; thank your friends and family for the help they have given to you. Be grateful, you are safe. Say thank you to the Angels in your life.

Intention:
I am protected by my Guardian Angel.

The Message and You:
You are safe.

ANGELS

You are safe

BEAUTIFUL

I am beautiful.

We are all guilty of telling ourselves what we are not.

There is lots of fear and negativity around us daily. It's in our workplaces, neighborhoods, schools, and on our televisions.

The negative influences we are exposed to at a very early age form some of our unconscious negative behavioral patterning and programming later in life. These sorts of conditions can be difficult to break free from.

We cannot run from it; yet we can reprogram and recondition our minds to a higher state of being, to deal with it all positively.

Here is some food for your mind.

Whenever you feel down on yourself or your life:
STOP - change your thinking!

You are a perfect being with a perfect healthy body. You are beautiful. You are wealthy. You are safe. You are amazing. You are in a beautiful harmonious relationship. You are empowered. You are living your dream.

**Intention:
I instill positive intentions within my life. I am perfectly Me.**

The Message and You:
You are Magnificent.

BEAUTIFUL

You are Magnificent

BELIEVE

Believe in yourself

Self-belief; do you have it or do you not?

Do you 'second guess' yourself or doubt yourself?
Do you go with your first thought or second thought?
Do you continually ask others to choose for you or follow their opinion?

This demonstrates a lack of self-belief; a lack of self-trust. Do not let your fear of failure - or fear of success - get in the way of your greatness.

You have the power to change your current circumstances. It begins with just one thought. Like attracts like; water finds its own level. That first positive thought will attract similar, positive thoughts.

Follow up that productive thought with an action. Stand up and walk forward – take one step at a time. Take another action, take another step forward and before you know it, you will be off and running!
The seemingly impossible becomes possible.

Sometimes we go though our whole life searching for something, someone, a place, a way of life; anything that might fulfill us.

"I too have spent my life searching. I was able to find what I was searching for. It was right here the whole time - it was me!"

One person has the power to change the lives of many.

Intention:
I believe in myself. I can create anything I want.

The Message and You:
You are that that you seek.

BELIEVE

You are that that you seek

BOUNDARIES

I have strong boundaries.

It is very important to set clear, strong boundaries, with yourself and with others. Setting clear boundaries with all the people in your life helps you and also helps them.
They will know precisely where they stand within the relationship you share, and it is easier to honor each other.

Clear, strong boundaries will also help you to relate to many people simultaneously; without any confusion or mixed signals.

Be very clear with people; let them know where they stand in your world.

It is very important for you to be open and honest about your boundaries with your loved ones.
These are the people who support you and love you unconditionally - in most cases these are the people who share their lives with you. They stand by you in the hard times and the good times. As you address your boundaries together, your relationship takes on a new life and direction.

Allow the boundaries you have around yourself and others to change as you change.

**Intention:
I express my relationship to others openly.**

The Message and You:
You are at peace with yourself and others.

BOUNDARIES

You are at peace with yourself and others

CELEBRATION

Pop open the Champagne bottle, Time to have a party!

You have worked so hard to achieve your goals. You have worried, you have struggled, had sleepless nights, gone through the pain, the suffering, the sacrificing. You came so very close to giving up, on many occasions, but you didn't.

Guess what!? Hooray! Hooray! You have done it! You have achieved your goals! Celebrate; give yourself a pat on the back - well done!

Be thankful to all those who have helped you get where you are. Some have played a large part, some small, but all of them have helped you achieve your goals - even the ones that caused you misery once! Be thankful to them as their misery helped make you stronger.

To help you celebrate, break up your goals into small steps. Count how many you have achieved already. Celebrate all the little steps in your life.

Each step counts.

**Intention:
I understand the importance of Celebration.
Hip hip hooray! Hip hip hooray!**

The Message and You:
You are having the time of your life!

CELEBRATION

You are having the time of your life!

CHILDREN

Look at life through the eyes of a child.

What happens to our children when they grow into adults? Do the circumstances of life change them, or do they become trapped within their own fears, doubts, worries and self-inflicted fear-based programming?

Children have no fears or hang-ups. They are bold, beautiful and carefree; full of life, joyful and playful in each moment.

Make peace with any conflicts you have with yourself, your family or friends. Restore balance and tranquility to your life.

Take full responsibility for your actions. If you take responsibility for all your actions, it stops the blame game. You cultivate and nurture your own empowerment.

You are free to be yourself.

You become real and honest about your life choices.
The simplest of joys and wisdom return to you.

**Intention:
I embrace my carefree nature.**

The Message and You:
You are joyful and playful.

CHILDREN

You are joyful and playful

CHOICES

Let's go shopping, what shall we buy? You have choices.

We all go shopping; at the local supermarket for groceries and home wares, or at the large department store to purchase new clothes or electrical appliances. We also have major purchases - a new house, a new car or a holiday.

What will you choose? You have many options.

You also choose the people you share your life with.
Your neighbors, friends, family, work associates, college and school friends. You may decide to move interstate, get married, change jobs; these are all life-changing events which will immensely alter your perception and experience of life.

Your choices are life-changing. You have free will.

You are free to live your life as you choose. There are no wrongs or rights here, just life experiences.

Choose the life experiences which bring you the most joy. Your joyful choices will bring lots of smiles to all those connected to you.
You get to create the best life experiences. The choice is yours.

**Intention:
At the crossroads of life, I choose the road that brings me the most joy.
I choose my experiences.**

The Message and You:
You are welcome to choose whatever life experience you wish to have.

CHOICES

You are welcome to choose whatever life experience
you wish to have

DANCE

The ballerina graces your presence today.

Where are your thoughts today? Do you always think about tomorrow? Is your mind always on your future? Or are you continuously thinking about yesterday, the past of you.
Ask yourself; are you in life, or do you watch life go by? Be the wheel, don't watch the wheel. It's a bit like going to a school dance, do not sit and watch whilst others dance - take a partner and dance the night away.

Dance and sing to the rhythm of life!

Dance a little, sing a little, smile a little, and be in this moment.
For this moment is all there is. Yesterday has gone, tomorrow is yet to come, the moment now is all there is.

Be aware of where your attention is, it matters.
Take your attention and put it into the now.

The power of now is profound, as all your creations are created in this now moment. This present moment holds the key to all things.

Intention:
I embrace and love the dance of life.

The Message and You:
You are an integral part of life.

DANCE

You are an integral part of life

DREAMS

Live your dreams!

Awaken your passion! What are you really passionate about? What brings you joy and excitement?

If you recognize you have no passion attached to your dreams, ask yourself why that is? Do not be afraid to dream, we all have dreams; work towards them and make them your reality!

If you are deeply passionate about your dreams, you will manifest these things very quickly in your life. Now, this may be a good time to change your dreams into something you are passionate about.

Dream big and then set them in motion. Go for it, follow your vision! Take the first step and then take another step, and then the next. Keep the larger picture in mind.

It is not about the pot of gold at the end of the rainbow, but about the journey and adventure taking place along the way.

Look at all the people you meet along the way, look at all the things you learn and experience.

Remember - the tallest buildings began with just one brick. Each brick laid brings the building closer to completion. Each step you take brings you closer to your dream.

GO FOR IT.

Intention:
I live my Dream. Dreams come true for me.

The Message and You:
You are living your dream.

DREAMS

You are living your dream

EARTH

I love Mother Earth for it is my home.

Listen to Mother Earth, she speaks to you: "Help me! Help me!" her cries echo through the lands.

Mother Earth is going through many vibrational changes which are already affecting everyone and everything that resides on this beautiful planet of ours.

Take time out to connect with Mother Earth; go for a bush walk. Unite with the wisdom of the old trees, be one with the wild life. Take your shoes off and walk through the park. Inhale the scent of the flowers and soak in the magnificence of Mother Earth. Breathe in the fragrance of the outdoors. Go for a swim in the ocean, walk along the beach, watch the whales and listen to the waves as they reach for the shore.

**Notice where your attention goes:
Mother Earth may be giving you an insightful message.**

We all need to play our part; conserve water, switch to more energy efficient products, collect rain water, save our natural resources, look after our native animals, watch over our rivers and our oceans. Get actively involved on a community level.
Recycle your garbage, use ozone friendly products, or perhaps join a tree planting group.

Together, we can move mountains.

**Intention:
I am sensitive to the needs of Mother Earth.**

The Message and You:
You are the caretaker of Mother Earth.

EARTH

You are the caretaker of Mother Earth

FINGERPRINTS

You touch the lives of many.

You leave your energetic imprint on the people in your life, as they leave theirs on you.
Now, if both parties were to leave a positive, helpful, joyful imprint on each other this would be wonderful; but this is not always the case.

Sometimes you will find that people leave such a negative energetic imprint on you that it may scar you for many years; long after the person in question has left your life.

Close your eyes, focus on seeing white light around yourself, notice if there are any black spots; these represent the negative energetic fingerprints that other people have left on you.

Now, imagine yourself cleaning these black spots using a golden cloth. It is a bit like cleaning the windscreen on your car. Once you are done, it is much easier to see where you are going and, you are less likely to create an unpleasant and unwanted experience.

Think about all the positive joyful experiences that you have shared with others. These are the best energetic imprints to remember and recreate. These wonderful experiences will form a fantastic springboard for your life.

**Intention:
I create positive imprints for myself and others.**

***The Message and You:*
You are free.**

FINGERPRINTS

You are free

FORGIVENESS

I love and forgive myself.

Sometime we do and say things which we regret.
Forgive yourself, forgive others.
Do not be afraid to say sorry or thank you.
Take responsibility for your actions.

Complete what you begin, do not leave things in limbo.
See it through or let it go.

How does one overcome doubt in one's life? Is it a lack of self-confidence, the absence of faith, or merely the fear of failure?

Be clear in your mind, face your doubts. Hold your head up high and be proud of the person you have become.

Be graceful in your actions, be loving, be thankful, and be forgiving. This will make an enormous difference in your life. It will cause your relationship with others and yourself to blossom.

Forgiveness is a blessing from the Self to the self.

**Intention:
I forgive and forget.**

The Message and You:
You are forgiven.

FORGIVENESS

You are forgiven

FRIENDSHIPS

Friends for life, friends forever.

Some friendships come and go, while others stay with you always.

Friendship means being there for each other; supporting each other through thick and thin, in joy and sorrow, in life and in death.

Be a good friend, be a good listener. Friends count on each other, depend on each other. A good friend is someone who makes time for you, understands you, and is considerate towards your needs.

Share your life with others, don't separate yourself. Be a witness to each other's lives. We all learn so many different wonderful things from each other. Be kind and sensitive towards each other.

Some friendships will stay with you your whole life. But life does change and so do people. Some friends will come and soon go and that is okay. For we are all forever changing.

**Intention:
I move with the winds of change.
I am a loving, considerate, understanding friend.**

The Message and You:
You are the best friend anyone could ever have.

FRIENDSHIPS

You are the best friend anyone could ever have

HEALING

For those who wish to be healed.

Sometimes our bodies get very sick and unwell.
Sometimes our bodies get so ill that we are unable to see beyond our pain, let alone contemplate the possible reasons for our illness.

Yet, if your body is crippled with disease or is continuously ill or suffers from an emotional dysfunction, ask yourself:
"Am I doing this to myself? Or is it my fate?"

Just for a moment, contemplate the possibility that your body is merely a vehicle that you utilize in your human journey on earth. And that your bad health or illness is merely one of your unconscious creations which you have not yet taken full responsibility for, but you can at any moment.

Now give your body a new command to heal...

I am perfect divine health.

This will begin to reprogram your body, telling it "It is time to heal." Your healing process has begun now. It is up to you to have faith and follow the messages and guidance that the Universe presents to you. This is part of your life experience, do not despair – you will get through it.

So heal that body. Heal that mind.

**Intention:
I am my own healer.**

***The Message and You:*
You are Perfect Divine body.**

HEALING

You are Perfect Divine body

HEALTH

I am happy, healthy and full of life.

Your body is a temple, look after it.
Be kind to it and it will be kind to you.

Be aware of the different foods you eat, be aware of the different journeys your food takes to get to you. This has an effect on your well-being and how your body feels.

A healthy body means a healthy mind. Look in the mirror, ask yourself, "Do I like how I look? Do I like myself?" Be honest. There are no prizes for tricking yourself. If you do not like your physical body, then do something about it. Begin new healthy eating habits, research different foods; study their effects on the body.

Free your mind of negative, unsupportive thoughts Imagine your mind is a garden and the negative thoughts are merely weeds in that garden. Pull the weeds out, this will allow beautiful thoughts to manifest in you.

Listen to your body as it knows what you need.

Intention:
I am a conscious, healthy, youthful person.

The Message and You:
You are Perfect Divine health.

HEALTH

You are Perfect Divine health

HEART

My heart is open.

Are you are thinker, or a doer? Do you watch life or, are you into life?
Are you in your head, or are you in your heart?
Or, do you have balance?
Ask yourself these questions; it will help you unlock yourself from your past conditioning.

We all look into our hearts at different times in our lives. Have you ever fallen in love? Had your heart broken by someone? Lost someone dear to you in your life? Experienced the end of a relationship, or the loss of a loved one?

Loss of love is a big one for the heart to get over. This can be very, very difficult and painful. Sometimes people keep reliving past misery and are unable to change their thoughts, which drag them back to their past misery. If so, ask for help.

Remember that your heart does heal. You do move on; it is okay to pause when needed, but do not keep reliving the memory of a past loss. It is okay to let others help, and be there for you. Give yourself time, be patient and loving towards yourself, time will heal the heart.

Your heart is the doorway to your life. Open your heart and feel life through your heart centre.

Intention:
My heart is healed.

The Message and You:
You are okay, your heart is open.

HEART

You are okay, your heart is open

HOLIDAY

**Goodbye, farewell! We'll see you later!
We're going on holiday!**

Excitement is in the air! The jostling, the shouts of laughter, the anticipation! The buzz of expectation surrounds us!

Let yourself go! Be free like a bird, soaring through the air!

Let go of the chatter and worry that you have in your mind. This is time for time out! This is what you need. Have a break, have a nice long warm bath. Pamper yourself, you deserve it.

If you continually burn the candle at both ends, you will burn out and fall in a heap.

If you are the sort of person who continually does this to yourself, ask yourself,
"Why am I doing this?"

Take time out. Have a break.

Make time for yourself. It's important for your state of mind and your well-being.

**Intention:
I take time out to pamper myself.**

The Message and You:
You are going on an overseas trip.

HOLIDAY

You are going on an overseas trip

HONESTY

I am honest with myself. I am honest with others.

It is very important for you to know what you intrinsically believe about yourself.

Are you honest with yourself? Are you honest with others? Ask yourself these questions.

If you are thinking you are honest when you are not, it will affect your life in a negative, unproductive way. You will always find dead ends and never know why.

Remember your life is a reflection of what you are thinking; your thoughts create your reality, whether you are conscious of it or not.

Be honest with your thoughts and feelings, towards yourself and others.

Life will present you with many wonderful life experiences to learn from, so that you see what you were not seeing before.

An honest mind is able to see beyond its own self-limiting deception; increasing one's sense of self-belief, instilling confidence and courage.

Intention:
I honor myself and others, with honesty.

The Message and You:
You are honest with yourself and others.

HONESTY

You are honest with yourself and others

HOPE

The light of hope shines so brightly.

We all lead busy lives; we do not seem to have time for the little pleasures of life anymore.

There is much confusion and despair in the world today - so many people appear to have lost their way. People give up on themselves far too easily. We can become lost within ourselves, turning our backs on the people who are genuinely trying to help us. Hope goes out the door very quickly.

However, hope never disappears; hope is always there, hope always offers you the possibility of changing a seemingly impossible situation.

Do not give up on yourself. You are brilliant! You just need to see your own brilliance.

Focus on all the good things in your life. You are loved and people do care for you, even if you do not feel it at times.

Trust your inner feelings; follow your 'inner knowing'.
You know what to do.

Just go for it, hope will show you the way.

**Intention:
I am forever hopeful.**

The Message and You:
You are guided by the light of hope.

HOPE

You are guided by the light of hope

JOY

Life is too short,
Be happy, be joyous

We seem to take life so seriously; we worry too much, think too much, let the present cloud our minds too much.
If we continuously worry about all the things that have not happened in our lives; it can cause much disarray, confusion and disharmony in our physical world.
Life then turns into a game of survival: Can we pay the rent? Do we have money for food? Where is the money for petrol? Why me? Why me? When did life become so difficult?

STOP. Change your thinking; replace your worrying thoughts with happy ones. Recall all the good times. Re-live your happy memories. If you wish to change your current circumstances or state of mind, start thinking different thoughts.

Give your mind a new reality-creating statement.
I am wonderful. I have everything I need. I am fulfilled.

Can it be this easy? Yes it can be. So turn your life into a joyous game: think joy, be joy. Joy brings more joy. It is contagious. Remember, your mind is like your own personal genie. Feed it joyful, happy thoughts and it gives you love, joy, happiness and lots of laughter.

You shall reap what you sow.

Intention:
I choose joy in my life.

The Message and You:
You are joyous.

JOY

You are joyous

KNOWLEDGE

I am forever learning new things.

My knowledge of myself, others and Life itself, is forever expanding.

High school, college, university: These are all places of learning.

Expand your mind, learn new concepts, and be open to new possibilities.
Commitment to your education is important.

You will meet and have many teachers throughout your life. Think about all the different people in your life. Some are there to teach you; others are there for you to teach them.

Different people turn up at different times in life to play the teacher's role for you. They come to help you learn some of life's more challenging lessons that are difficult to learn on your own.

So listen, and learn these life lessons well; for the day will soon come when Life will ask you to be the teacher.

**Intention:
I am a gatherer of knowledge.**

The Message and You:
You are forever learning and exploring.

KNOWLEDGE

You are forever learning and exploring

LAUGHTER

Laugh at yourself!

It is time to laugh! Laughter is the best medicine you will ever find.

Loosen up, and look for the laughter and the joy in all things. You can light the world with your smile.

If you cannot find a reason to bring laughter into your life, or find a reason to smile - then do something about it! Join a laughter group!

Get involved; surround yourself with positive, uplifting and joyous people. The company you choose to keep can have an uplifting or dampening effect on you. Which will you choose?

Make a conscious decision to laugh each day. The more laughter you bring into your life, the lighter you become within yourself. You will find that your physical health and physical life will also change for the better.

A happy mind brings happy thoughts. This is what the best life experiences are really about... happiness.

Intention:
I am blessed with the gift of laughter.

The Message and You:
You are spontaneous.

LAUGHTER

You are spontaneous

LOOSE ENDS

Tie up all your loose ends.

You may be asking yourself; what are loose ends?
Perhaps they are people you never really got to know; or unfinished business you never quite completed.

Think about all your incomplete relationships, unresolved issues, the people you have left behind and also those that left you in 'Limboland'.

You see, loose ends affect your ability to move forward - both in your personal and business life. These old connections and unresolved issues have your fixed attention trapped within them.

Tie up your loose ends, the rewards are exhilarating.

Start making a list of such people and instances: personal and professional affairs. It does not matter how long or short your list is. You must be honest with yourself, this is important for you.

As you resolve your loose ends - and it does not take long – it has an extraordinary affect on you. It will increase your focus, and the extra positive energy that you will have available to you, will help in the achievement of your deepest heart desires.
Great news - one leads to another and you begin
a snow-ball affect.

Be bold, be brave.

**Intention:
I live my life as a free spirit.**

***The Message and You:*
You are free to create new experiences.**

LOOSE ENDS

You are free to create new experiences

LOVE

Love yourself.

So many people go through life not liking themselves. Why does one do this to one's self? How can others love you if are unable to love yourself? Would you treat your best friend like this?

Ask yourself, do you like yourself? Do you love yourself?
Listen to the answers. If there are negative responses to your questions - do something about it. If there is something you dislike about yourself - do something about it. Turn your negative responses into positive actions - it really is that simple.

Love who you are!

Look inside your heart, feel the unique person you are, smile at yourself, smile at life. Life smiles back! You can exercise, eat healthy foods and join a support group. The hardest thing about change is taking the first step, the rest is history.

Intention:
I am a more loving, caring, accepting, understanding, compassionate human being.
I love and accept myself for who I am.

The Message and You:
You are loved unconditionally.

LOVE

You are loved unconditionally

LOVERS

I am in love with you.

True love always finds a way of bringing two people together.

Haven't we all heard the phrases: "We found each other, it happened so quickly." "It was destiny!"

Do not look for love. Let it find you. If you are already with someone then you are with who you are meant to be with.

Sometimes people wonder if they are with the right person, or will they ever find true love? "Yes, yes," I say.

There are no rights or wrongs here. There is always a beautiful learning and healing that takes place within an intimate relationship, even though you may not see it this way at the time.

Be honest and loving, have an open heart, be willing to understand one another's viewpoint, be forgiving and supportive. Make a commitment to be there for each other.

Do not be afraid to fall in love. The deep love one finds within a close relationship is truly one of life's greatest gifts.

**Intention:
I am thankful for the love I have found / of the love that finds me.**

The Message and You:
You are in love.

LOVERS

You are in love

MAGIC

Magic is in the air.

Let me sprinkle you with my magical Angel Dust!

Magic is more than the magic you see in birthday parties! It is everywhere around you - you yourself are magic and create magic!

When you use your passion, pursue your dreams, channel your positive energy; you create magic!

When you honor others, are accepting, allow hope to design your dreams, and move on, further and further, you create magic!

Be brave, be strong, you have the power and ability to manifest your heart's desires in your life.

Be true to yourself, live a joyous and driven life, laugh a lot, fly like an eagle, make magic happen!

Intention:
I am the magician, I create magic!

The Message and You:
You are your own magician.

MAGIC

You are your own magician

MUSIC

I can hear the music…sing and dance the night away!

Music has a special way of unlocking your deepest, unfelt feelings.

Turn on the radio, listen to the music. Listen to your 'heart song' - the song that resonates most with your deepest self. Allow yourself to hear and feel the music profoundly, this helps you.
It opens your heart.

You must be aware of your feelings. They define you. You experience many feelings through the day, and a lot more throughout your whole life. Learn to interpret your feelings, keep them alive!

As you expand your heart centre, this increases your level of self-trust. It raises your vibration to a higher state of being. You become much softer, lighter and more accepting of people.

Music has an un-caging effect. It awakens much more joy and love in your daily life.

Feel the music, feel the rhythm of life. Sing hearty songs, be joyful, have fun, laugh a lot.

Intention:
I am in touch with my feelings.

The Message and You:
You are a loving, giving human being who is in touch with their feelings and emotions.

MUSIC

You are a loving, giving human being who is in touch with their feelings and emotions.

MYSTERIES

There is so much that is unknown to us.

Gaze over the ocean on a beautiful summer day. It is so vast, beautiful, endless and timeless. There is much we do not know about it.

The ocean holds so many secrets and mysteries. In this way, it reflects life so beautifully.

You too are like the ocean, vast, beautiful, limitless and timeless. You too hold many mysteries and treasures within you that await your discovery.

The Self is a rich bounty, waiting to be revealed. The Self carries the magic to all things, and it is only found in the now, the present. Be present in this now moment; look upon your current reality and make a decision to change what no longer serves you.

Move on with your life. Get back into the magic of living in the moment.

Intention:
I am my own greatest mystery.

The Message and You:
You are present in this moment; the wonders of life are r evealed to you.

MYSTERIES

You are present in this moment; the wonders of life
are revealed to you

NEW BEGINNINGS

New opportunities come your way.

Be open to new opportunities - the Universe is always opening new doors for you. This happens whether or not you are aware of it;

and whether or not you grasp the new opportunities,

as and when they come.

Life also shows you new paths to walk on. It allows new people to come in and out of your life.

Normally it is your fears that stop you moving forward. Your fears may show up in different ways: lack of knowledge, knowhow or courage. It is okay to have fears, and it is also normal to have worries or concerns about beginning something new. However, when this happens to you, instead of letting your doubts rule your life; just *pause*.

Take a moment. Recognize it is just one of your fears saying hello to you. Simply acknowledge its presence and move on towards your new venture with a positive outlook.

If you miss one opportunity, be assured that there is another one waiting for you around the corner. Be open to additional possibilities, embrace the new.

Intention:
I am open to new opportunities.

The Message and You:
You are entering a new stage in your life.

NEW BEGINNINGS

You are entering a new stage in your life

PETS

My pet is my companion.

We love our pets so deeply and whole-heartedly, we can learn so much from our animals.

They teach us so many beautiful things about ourselves. They teach how to love unconditionally, how to accept ourselves, and love each other.

We learn how to give and receive love without expectation, we learn about relationships. We love our pet animals, treat them and care for them as they are part of our family. This is beautiful.

Go for a walk in the park, listen to all the animals. You see the birds sing songs of joy to you, the dog speaks to you about friendships, the Kookaburra laughs at you and says, "Lighten up, stop being so serious about yourself! It is a beautiful day; put a smile on your face! Life smiles at you."

**Intention:
I embrace the beauty in all things.**

***The Message and You:*
You are loved.**

PETS

You are loved

PROSPERITY

I reap the rewards of my labors; I pick the fruits I have sown.

Whatever you choose to do or be in your life; work hard for it, be committed.

Realize that when you work hard and commit to something - whether it is a relationship, friendship, work, business, study, family or any other project - you are the one who will reap the rewards.

When the going gets tough, call upon your courage and strength; get outside help if required.

Never give up on yourself, be strong, be bold and walk forward.

You are the master of your own destiny. Excuses breed excuses, good fortune breeds good fortune. Plant beautiful thoughts in your mind - beautiful thoughts grow into wonderful intentions which then manifest themselves into incredible life experiences.

Intention:
I am prosperous.

The Message and You:
You are successful in all areas of your life.

PROSPERITY

You are successful in all areas of your life

PUZZLE PIECES

We have all these different pieces and nothing fits.
Or do they?

Life is made up of many different pieces of a puzzle - work, family, friends and relationships. We try to work everything out before we have the experience.

We more often than not pre-judge people, things and places; we decide the outcome before we have the experience.

You may take a new job or move interstate or get married. These are all life-changing events; you may not be able to see how your old life fits with your new life. Let go of your need to know what tomorrow brings. Trust that what you are creating for tomorrow fits you today.

Begin with two pieces that fit together. Trust in Life itself to show you the big picture. It may well turn out to be more incredible than your deepest, most heartfelt dreams.

Be a witness to your life.

Life is forever changing and so are you. Learn to be flexible. Flow with life like a graceful swan gliding through the water on a beautiful summer's day.
In the end, it will all fit in. In the end, you will complete your life.

Intention:
I will make the most of my life.

The Message and You:
You are complete.

PUZZLE PIECES

You are complete

REFLECTIONS

I am able to see the past Me and the Me of today.

Take a moment and sit. Be still, let go of the chatter in your head. Reflect on today's events. Review your life from your birth to this moment. Evaluate the choices you have made.

What do you see?

What you are seeing has caused your life to become what it is. Ask yourself: "Am I happy and content; or is it otherwise?"

You have the power and ability to change yourself and your life; it begins in this very moment. Be very clear with yourself.
What is it that you want from life? What brings you the greatest joy?

Be honest with yourself, and then in that moment make a decision to change yourself and your life. Be strong, be brave and just do it.

You have the ability to make a difference.

**Intention:
I have the ability to change my life. I decide.**

The Message and You:
You are insightful.

REFLECTIONS

You are insightful

RELATIONSHIPS

Are you in a relationship or are you single?

If you are in a relationship, whether you are married, de facto or boy-friend/girlfriend, matters not. This is the time to reflect on your relationship: Are you in love with one another? Are you open and honest with each other? Are you committed to each other? Are you a loving, caring forgiving, understanding partner? Does your partner reflect these virtues to you?

If you wish to be in a relationship, and are not; ask yourself: Do you love the unique being you are? Are you open and honest with yourself? What commitments do you have to yourself? What are your values and virtues?

Pose yourself these questions. Your answers will help you better understand yourself and others - be honest with yourself.

There are so many people in our lives that we interact with each and every day. Think about all the different relationships you currently have in your life. Be kind and loving to all those close to you, it is okay to let go of the relationships that no longer support you in a loving way.

The most important relationship you will ever have is the one you have with yourself.

Be kind, loving and understanding of your own needs and wants. This is a key to having a joyous life. Live life as best as you possibly can. Make the most of it, be good to yourself, and to your fellow man.

Intention:
I am loving, supportive and understanding of my own wishes and desires.

The Message and You:
You are your own best friend.

RELATIONSHIPS

You are your own best friend

RESPECT

I have honor and respect for who I am in this world. I have honor and respect for others. For this is who I am.

We cannot speak or act for others; one must honor and respect the decisions of others. Each person is inherently independent in his/her own choices.

It is not our place to decide what is best for another; sometimes we get confused between caring for someone and trying to control someone.

This controlling nature of ours is based on fear. This fear can be anything, fear of being controlled, fear of loss, fear of failure, fear of judgment. Only once we learn to recognize these fears in ourselves will we recognize it in others, and realize they are much the same as us.

Respecting others means we understand and respect ourselves.

Intention:
I accept and respect the wishes and decisions of others.

The Message and You:
You are in acceptance of the journeys of others.

RESPECT

You are in acceptance of the journeys of others

SCHOOL

You are enrolled in the school of life.

We begin our education at a very early age; our school is a very big part of our life. On average we spend approximately fifteen to twenty years of our time educating ourselves.

But does our learning stop there? Or does it continue for the rest of our lives? You leave your classroom teachers as you complete your formal education.

School is still in and life itself is your teacher!

There are many people with whom you relate to each and every day. You will find that some of these people are your informal teachers, so listen well to what they say to you.

Imagine every experience, every moment you have had until now, and every future experience you will have – it is all part of your education.

You may ask yourself: "What is it that I am learning? What is my life teaching me?

Patience, honesty, self-belief, how to love oneself, respect, honor, humility, self-trust, forgiveness, joy, happiness, to have faith, togetherness, friendships, commitment - these are just some of the lessons life will teach you.

Do you get the idea? Enjoy your life, enjoy the wonderful education it provides; the lessons are with you for eternity.

Intention:
I am intelligent.

The Message and You:
You are the student, life is your teacher.

SCHOOL

You are the student, life is your teacher

SHARING

Sharing is caring.

Have you wanted something, seen it every day but then gone home without it? Not by choice, but by circumstance? Do you know what going without feels like?

Why do more people go without? Why is this so? There is no need for it. There is more than enough food, clothing and money to go around for all that live on Planet Earth.

We must wake up! Help each other care for one other, love each other; you must lend a hand when you can. Help someone less fortunate than yourself. Just giving someone a smile may help that person get through the day.

Be there for your fellow man; we all fall on hard or difficult circumstances. These are a part of life. So we must be there for each other.

Support your brothers and sisters. Sharing your life with others gives you a greater sense of belonging. At the end of the day, we are all family.

**Intention:
I support my fellow man.**

The Message and You:
You are a loving caring, individual.

SHARING

You are a loving caring, individual

STRENGTH

I have inner strength.

Sometimes we allow our fears to consume us. The fears we encountered as children are the fears we more often than not carry into our adult lives. These fears are like trances; like parental programs that are running in the background of our minds.

You are unaware of their existence only because they were created by you at an early age, to cope with an event or occurrence. Different life experiences will trigger some of these fears and cause them to show themselves and threaten to consume you.

Whenever you become fearful of someone or something, pause for a moment and question why you are fearful. The answer to your question may release you from a past trauma which has being affecting you for your whole life.

You will then feel empowered. This has a liberating effect on you.

Remember, there is a reason for everything that happens to you in your life.

Intention:
I am strong because I am no longer afraid.

The Message and You:
You are empowered.

STRENGTH

You are empowered

SURPRISE

Surprise! Surprise! Guess what? Guess who? Surprise!

Life is full of surprises. You never know what you will get or who you will meet.

Let fate and destiny play its part in your life. Be open to all possibilities. Sometimes we think we know what tomorrow brings but we do not.
For it is the unknown. It has not yet happened.

Take a chance on life; follow your intuitive feelings, your inner knowing. Anything is possible, let go, dream a little and go for it.

Stand tall take a deep breath.

Today is a new day. Be spontaneous, who knows what today brings.

Allow life to surprise you.

**Intention:
I live in the now, I lovingly accept and receive the unforeseen gifts of life.**

The Message and You:
You are so happy.

SURPRISE

You are so happy

TEACHER

Are you the student? Or are you the teacher? Or are you both?

You will have many teachers throughout your life. The most unlikely people may turn out to be your greatest teachers.

There is so much we can learn from each other. Our lives are more often than not connected to so many other people of different walks of life. Listen well, pay attention; school is in and Life itself is your greatest teacher.

We cannot help but learn from each other - it is all such a beautiful exchange. If you are able to reflect on your life in this manner you will begin to realize that all of your relationships are perfect – just the way they are.

Take time to reflect back on past relationships:
What did you learn? And are you able to put this new knowledge, these new insights, into action? Bring it all forward into your new relationships. Stop repeating old, bad habits.

The student becomes the teacher; and the apprentice becomes the master.

A new learning, the light of a new understanding enters your mind.

Intention:
I am aware of my teachers.

The Message and You:
You are open to new ways of thinking.

TEACHER

You are open to new ways of thinking

TRANSFORMATION

Move with the winds of change.

With each new moment, each new experience, your knowledge grows. Your mind expands and your fear of the unknown lessens. You take full responsibility for your actions; you begin to realize that there is a reason for everything that happens in your life - the 'you of yesterday' transforms into the 'you of today'.

As you change, things around you also change.

Your outside world is always a reflection of your inside world. The winds of change are always around you. The trees lose their leaves, the snow falls on the mountains, and sun shines on the green valleys. You too begin a new relationship, travel abroad, you begin something new.

Don't resist change; learn to be flexible. Move with the winds of change like a willow tree on a breezy, summer's day.

Intention:
I am open to new viewpoints.

The Message and You:
You are forever changing.

TRANSFORMATION

You are forever changing

TRUST

I trust in me.

Trust is like knowing that everything is going to be alright, it is an inner knowing. It is a feeling intrinsic to your heart.

But how does one get to this point?

Begin with getting in touch with your inner feelings:
What are you feeling? Why do you feel that way?

Learn to trust your inner feelings, your instinctive knowing; this is the inner you showing you the right way to go.

Remember this, my friend - the one thing that will stop you from embracing your inner feelings are your fears.

If you can be honest with yourself about the fears you have in different areas of your life, then this is a major realization. This alone will help you immensely in your ability to having a greater level of self-trust.

Intention:
I am one with my inner self, I follow my instincts.

The Message and You:
You are connected to your inner knowing.

TRUST

You are connected to your inner knowing

WISH

Your wish comes true.

Be grateful for what you have in your life. Give thanks for all the little things.

Be grateful for all the wonderful people who have been a part of your life, who have touched you so deeply. It was all meant to be, say thank you to your family and friends. Some people are with you always and love you unconditionally and some people are not there for you at all...and that is okay. It is all perfect, this is life.

Take a moment, be with the night sky.
Be with the vastness of all there is. Look up at all the stars twinkling away in the night sky.

You are part of all there is and you are that Genie you seek.

Make a wish it will come true - you are the creator of your own life. You have free will, there are no accidents. You created it all.

Your destiny lies in your own hands, think hard before you wish.

Intention:
I am my own destiny.

The Message and You:
You are the one who makes your wishes come true.

WISH

You are the one who makes your wishes come true

REMEMBER

You have the power to create miracles in your life.

You have been introduced to many new concepts and ideas; and new ways of looking at yourself, your life and the world around you.

At this point your mind may be in a spin. You may be challenged or confronted by these new concepts. But do not let them overwhelm you. Give it time for it all to sink in.

I have spoken of fear quite a bit through this text.
Fear is a big part of this world we live in. It is a fact of life.
Do not run from your fears or tell yourself you do not have any. Be honest with yourself. We all have fears – it is part of being human.

It takes great courage to recognize what you are afraid of and to accept that fear is present in you.

Recognition is the first step to accepting that fear and moving forward irrespective.

FOOD FOR YOUR MIND

Just trying to live life can be very difficult at times. Many events and situations occur throughout a person's life; sometimes we fall on hard times, sometimes we get lost, and sometimes we give up on ourselves and others. There are days where we are happy and full of life; and there are days where we are sad, angry and without hope:
"This is Life".

When you find yourself having a low day or it may be a difficult time in your life - this is the moment where you need to pause and take a deep breath. What belief or program do you have running which is creating this unwanted experience? Accept the experience you are having without judging it.

As you reach this point in your mind, give the mind a
new reality-creating statement.

You are loved or You are safe or You are forgiven or You are joyous. You choose the command that best suits your situation.

Doing this action will help you create the life you want to have.

You are welcome to have whatever life experience you wish to have - it is your choice.

It takes great courage to recognize what
you are afraid of.

The key is to accept that and move forward anyway.

Ross Bonacci

My life is an offering of Love

Ross Bonacci

Other Products from The Way Of The Soul

Soul Cards:

This beautifully illustrated 'The Way of the Soul' Soul Card set is Ross Bonacci's gift to you to honor and accelerate your journey home to yourself. Each card carries an Intention for you to feel at the core of your being like an inner compass. Easy to use and full of inspiration, this magical set of 42 cards and guidebook will transport you along the path to self empowerment. Ross proudly presents these cards to inspire and guide you through your travels with ease and grace. Your journey home to your self has begun, enjoy the journey of life. May the Cards and their sacred intentions be yours to treasure for a lifetime.

http://www.thewayofthesoul.com/index.php#/soul-cards/

Empowerment CD
Magic Happens CD
Reflections CD
http://itunes.apple.com/au/album/the-way-soul-magic-happens/id428834730

Majestic Journey Perpetual Calendar
A simple wall planner for writing down your own daily thoughts.
http://www.thewayofthesoul.com/index.php#/calander/

POST CARDS FROM THE VOID

"Take ownership of your dreams. You are the master of your own destiny."

ROSS BONACCI

Ross Bonacci, author / Founder of Way of the Soul brings you these eleven Post Cards from the Void to allow you to take a deeper look at the human condition and how we fit into the
 larger scheme of things.
http://www.amazon.com/s/ref=ntt_athr_dp_sr_1?_encoding=UTF8&sort=relevancerank&search-alias=books&field-author=Ross%20Bonacci

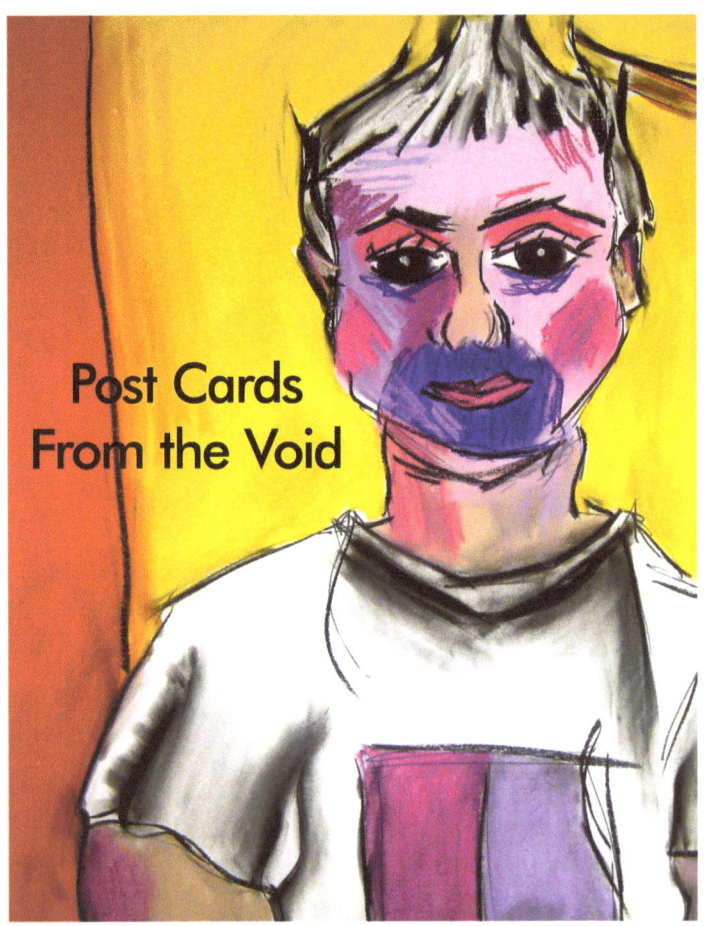

ROSS BONACCI

YOU ARE BEAUTIFUL

"YOU ARE BEAUTIFUL" is my gift to you to honor and accelerate your journey home to yourself. May this book guide you home with ease and grace. Enjoy the journey of life.

ROSS BONACCI

Ross Bonacci, author / Founder Way of the Soul brings you, YOU ARE BEAUTIFUL, a series of 42 insightful, thought provoking messages that promise to make you look deep inside to find inspiration and help you reach your goals.

The wonderful artwork will accentuate your experience of the allegories, mantras and positive statements in the messages.

Each message ends with a sacred intention for you to feel at the core of your
being like an inner compass.
http://www.amazon.com/s/ref=ntt_athr_dp_sr_1?_encoding=UTF8&sort=relevancerank&search-alias=books&field-author=Ross%20Bonacci

ROSS BONACCI

HOW TO CREATE INSTANT MAGIC IN A BUSY LIFE

INDEX

Adventure 9	Prosperity 71
Angels 11	Puzzle Pieces 73
Beautiful 13	Reflections 75
Believe 15	Relationships 77
Boundaries 17	Respect 79
Celebration 19	School 81
Children 21	Sharing 83
Choices 23	Strength 85
Dance 25	Surprise 87
Dreams 27	Teacher 89
Earth 29	Transformation 91
Fingerprints 31	Trust 93
Forgiveness 33	Wish 95
Friendships 35	
Healing 37	
Health 39	
Heart 41	
Holiday 43	
Honesty 45	
Hope 47	
Joy 49	
Knowledge 51	
Loose ends 55	
Love 57	
Lovers 59	
Magic 61	
Music 63	
Mysteries 65	
New beginnings 67	
Pets 69	

www.ingramcontent.com/pod-product-compliance
Lightning Source LLC
Chambersburg PA
CBHW040016240426
43664CB00038B/21